I0119069

RACE to the Finish

A Diversity and Inclusion Pocket Guide

Yesenia Peck MA

Copyright © 2020 Yesenia Peck

All rights reserved.

ISBN: 978-0-578-62932-2

DEDICATION

Eduardo Terreros-Ortiz and Matilde Leon-Cordero

Mom and Dad, Love you always!

.

CONTENTS

ACKNOWLEDGMENTS

Cover design

Designed by Freepik

INTRODUCTION

If you are reading this, chances are you are planning to include Diversity and Inclusion as a value in your community or organization. I commend you on your choice to begin this RACE. Organizations like yours who have taken steps to instill D&I have reported a number of benefits including happier employees and greater profits. While all organizations can benefit from Diversity and Inclusion, all will find different obstacles and tribulations in practice. The culture of some organizations and cultures are more amenable to D&I...for those of you who have found intransigence when trying to implement Diversity and Inclusion initiative...RACE to the Finish is for you.

All of us come from different places and have different cultural realities. Our recognition of diversity differs everywhere we go. Having lived in Nebraska for the past 15 years, the common refrain when I leave the two major cities in the state is that there is no diversity...that the state is overwhelmingly Caucasian. There are many problems with this thought but what is really being expressed is the believe that there is no ethnic diversity in Nebraska. This too is incorrect. When I came to work in Nebraska, I studied the demographics, I asked people who lived here. I was told, "There is no diversity in Nebraska." Come to find out that the Latino population statewide could easily fill the 3rd Largest city in

Nebraska…. University of Nebraska's Memorial Stadium. This doesn't even consider the other types of diversity that exist in the state.

While I do not think these kinds of ideas come from racism, they do come from a thought process that often makes people forget or at least fail to consider other groups in their midst because no one from these ethnic groups is in their social/personal orbit. While I cannot say for sure, cities like Detroit, MI at 80% African American, Honolulu, HI at 65% Asian and Laredo, TX at 95% Latino have similar thoughts from their residents. The real problem with this type of thinking is not race, it is staid, conservative thinking. A thought process that tends to make people believe that everyone thinks the way they do. In a community without diversity of thought…they probably do.

All communities and organizations are different. Your pathway to a successful inclusive community will have its own challenges, values and concerns. You may have a large Latino population, maybe you have a company with jobs that some don't deem appropriate for women, and maybe you have voices from the LGBT community that need to be heard. Whatever the mix you face it is easy to become overwhelmed at the idea of facing discord. That is what RACE to the Finish is all about. It is the blueprint from which you can customize your project to meet success.

This framework has served me well in my 15 years in the United States. I immigrated from Lima, Peru where I was an attorney with the Supreme Court of Peru. I found a community and a purpose working with the Nebraska Hispanic Chamber of Commerce in Omaha. Along the way I enhanced my education with a Master's in Leadership and a Graduate Certificate in Diversity and Inclusion from Cornell University. I have worked with communities all over the Midwest and have successfully used this program in all of them.

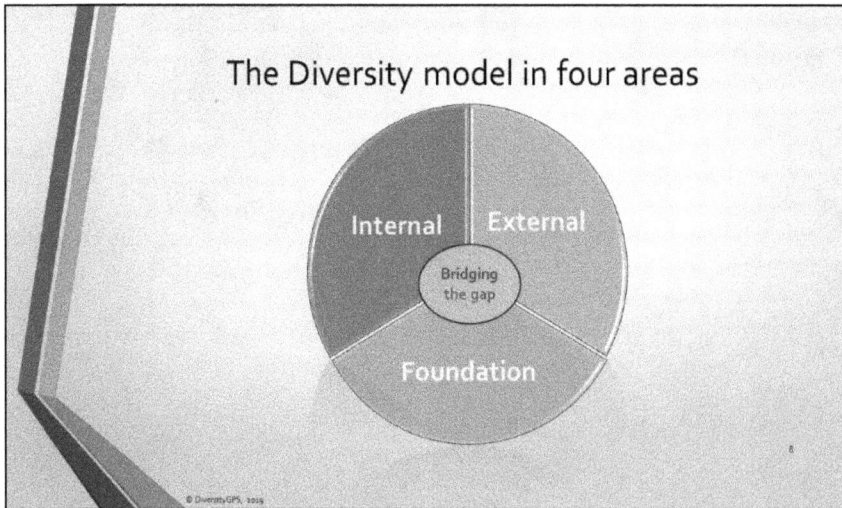

The Diversity model in four areas

Yesenia Peck, owner of DiversityGPS, created the Diversity diagram showing the harmonious relationship that must exist in a company's internal Diversity plan. It must be reflected in its external Diversity plan accompanied by a precise and uniform communication strategy. All must be built on a solid foundation of the business case for Diversity

All these plans are distinct and have different aims as to their end goals. They are all integrated based on a concept we call, "Bridging the Gap."

The Internal segment refers to the plan of action taken within the organization as it pertains to diversity and inclusion.

The External plan has to do with the actions an organization takes to transform the way customers and stakeholders think of the organization as it pertains to diversity and inclusion

The Foundation refers to the steps taken to bring diversity and

3

inclusion to the forefront in an organization and the community.

FOUNDATION: BUILDING THE FRAMEWORK

Diversity and Inclusion, like all worthwhile efforts, requires careful planning, review of your organization and perhaps most importantly a strong foundation. The strong foundation is where we make the business case for diversity. The business-case is why it make sense to create a diversity program. You might say to yourself that Diversity and Inclusion is just the right thing to do, but when you start looking into it, you will find that it tends to benefit the organization in various tangible ways as well. To have a solid and well- established foundation, it is important that executive management be the drivers of diversity and inclusion as values of the organization. This should be an explicit action of senior leaders rather than passive acknowledgement of the process.

Diversity must be recognized as an important value and position the responsibility for Diversity not merely with Human Resources department or Diversity offices, but with top-level and senior executives that must provide the visibility and commit the time and resources to make diversity happen. This may not be quickly realized by the entire company. Followed by a similar action or presentation by supervisory staff to their direct reports and on down the organizational chart.

Entering into a new organizational value requires a commitment by everyone to make it part of the culture. Organizational values are not like a light switch. It takes time and consistent effort to create the buy-in needed to effectively impart a value. When leadership recognizes diversity as an important goal and positions the responsibility for diversity with top-level and senior executives and not solely with human resource professionals.

When an organization begins this process in earnest, you will need to create a mission and vison that will guide your plan of action. Another aspect that is recommended is a set of expectations devoted to diversity from the executives. This can be a modified "Golden Rule," or a set of standards of behavior that become part of the culture of the organization. This step is optional and is based on the convictions of the individual organization.

Finally, the first phase will end with the development and implementation of an internal and external diversity plan.

THE INTERNAL PLAN

The internal plan refers to the actions that the organization takes to make sure that the firm can create sustainable diversity in their workforce.

The internal plan often starts with numerical history or data of the Diversity strategy of your company, but if Diversity is a fairly new item in your strategic plan, an internal climate survey is recommended. This is a survey or questionnaire that helps define what your organization knows about diversity, what they think of the concept and what level of diversity the firm already enjoys. A climate survey will offer a great deal of information to your plan of action.

While a climate survey has the benefit of offering new information, depending on how much time and effort has been taken to make sure diversity is imparted as a value into the organization, the results can be somewhat disheartening. There are a variety of different viewpoints that exist in public domain regarding the necessity of Diversity and Inclusion. These viewpoints are often political or closely held personal biases and will creep into the results.

In the end, your results will often tell you a whole host of things that you never expected. Even the results which are meant solely to be hostile to the process will reveal things that you would never respect. A good example of this comes from one of the surveys I performed. An employee late in his career was taking issue with most of the diversity questions that talked about race and gender. He was not impressed with the possibilities offered by diversity and it became an object of complaint. However, when the questions came to sexual orientation and age, the employee expressed a need to respect older employees and not reject them for younger recruits. The same responses came when he complained about the treatment he had endured as a homosexual in the organization. It was remarkable because it revealed that the employee did not really understand the depth and breadth of diversity and inclusion, but it also indicated honest feelings about what he as an employee felt about two distinct diversity segments.

When the climate survey results are compiled and analyzed, it will be very enlightening to see what your team thinks about the people around them. In rural and conservative areas without a great deal of diversity exposure, there may be rather extreme ideas. In my experience however, it is sometimes difficult to get some team members to display their true ideas due to a culture that advances amicability almost beyond most other virtuous traits.

The result of an initial survey is perhaps the most important part of the nascent D&I program. Results that show most of your workforce is adamantly opposed to a program may mean that you need to wait to add a diverse population to your organization. A climate survey that shows that your team is amenable to greater diversity tends to state that you can create a sustainable diversity program because you can attract and retain diverse employees. When sustainability seems likely, you are ready for the next phase.

Attract and retain talent

Recruiters often lament that a good worker is so hard to find. Maybe because you think that the job needs to be filled by a man, or a person of a particular generation, or maybe even a certain personality. When you give up looking for the perfect prototype it will probably be time to broaden your scope and admit you made your search too narrow. One of the great benefits of a Diversity and Inclusion program is it gets your team thinking about the vast array of who could possibly do the job for you. Diverse applicants don't just show up to apply, you have to ask them, you have to recruit the market you want.

How do we recruit the various diversity segments? It works a lot like marketing. Try and develop a plan on who you want to reach and how you can communicate with them. After you create a lucid plan then it comes down to the 4 "P" s of recruitment.

> **Position:** Using your plan of action, consider who you need for the position at hand. What recruiting sources would be best used for this type of position?

> **Pay:** This is another consideration that depends on the nature of the job as to how and where you identify your audience

> **Place:** Place can refer to internet advertising, campus employment assistance, temp agencies, or for the anachronistic, newspaper classifieds. Each of these places offer a connection to different diversity groups. When we think about each of these mediums, consider that any can be highly focused on a specific diversity segment. For example, I mentioned newspaper classified as an anachronism in jest. Newspapers are still a valid option for different generational segments and certainly for different ethnic diversity groups. Keep in mind that there are also websites that are specialized for nearly any diversity segment you can consider.

Promotion: How do you plan to promote the job? Are you translating the job into languages that will broaden your audience? Have you considered advertising and verbiage that appeals to the audience you are trying to reach? Once you can hire these new employees, how do you highlight and promote this to other potential employees.

Now that you are recruiting and have a plan to onboard a diverse new group of employees, keep in mind that some of your existing employees may take exception with your plan. That anti-diversity sentiment may rise. You may hear comments that work should got to the person that is the best person for the job. No one should get a job because they are of a certain ethnicity. When you hear this, agree with them! The reality is that you never hire any new employee simply because they fill a diversity bubble. Your diversity hire should fit the need and not be hired to check a box.

When the employer hires someone who is not as able to do a job and that ineptitude is identified, it creates a range of problems for both the employer and the employee. The employee will often be written off as a diversity hire which is often a concern anyway. Another problem with this is, the employee will often feel negative about the position because they are not finding success. Consequently, the employee may leave. Fellow employees who may already have some biases about diversity may look at the employee and suffer confirmation bias, which means that when they see anything that seems to confirm a preconceived notion will cause them to galvanize their biases even when new evidence seems to defy the beliefs.

Employers often suffer because all employees lose faith in management for weakening the team and creating derision. Employees may also get anxiety about diverse new hires because they feel their job is threatened by diversity interlopers. This decreases employee engagement and in time will increase employee turnover. While engaging in Diversity and Inclusion programs, it is necessary to maintain ethics and standards, even if you have created goals and are pressuring yourself to reach them. Better to fall short than lose integrity with all direct stakeholders.

Retention

Earlier we described that it was important to "feather the nest," to make the environment right for sustainable D&I hiring. The real reason behind all that is to insure retention. If we cannot maintain our new hires, if our churn rate is too high, we have not been successful. Retention when engaging in D&I means careful gardening.

Imagine walking into a building with a thousand other people and as you look around, you are the only one of your kind. You are the only black person, the only woman, the only Generation Z, the only person with a visible disability, you are simply the only one. How do you think you would feel? Where would you find support? This is the tricky situation with starting a D&I program where none had previously existed, you must try and cultivate from nothing a diverse team. Preferably, you will want to hire more than one of a diversity segments or make sure that you have multiple of different diversity segments so you can highlight your efforts to new hires.

Retention also depends on that earlier communication and reinforcement of company values. When your existing team is ready and comfortable for the diversity hires the new recruits can have comfortability with the groups that are already on the job. It also means that hopefully your new recruits will hear fewer comments and experience less negativity. That of course depends on how your organization promotes and reinforced Diversity and Inclusion as a value.

Development

Part of the concept of retention comes from developing or the opportunity for development. Diversity segments have a variety of different needs and interests, however, when the subject turns to development of employees, the youngest diversity segments in the workplace today, Millennials and Generation Z, both have interests in organizations with robust efforts at development. Development is an amalgam of several separate but interrelated concepts.

Perhaps one of the most important ways to promote development in your employees is to take individual interest them. This should start upon a job offer. The employer needs to identify the interests and goals of the new employee. When they start to work, it is so important to continue to meet with the new hire and work with them to help them meet their personal and career expectations. The new diversity hire will be more comfortable with a company that they feel they have a clear path through their career. It isn't just career planning that the diverse employee needs. Career advancement often means education.

Training and education are some of the most important concepts to new employees. Every job and career path can be approached differently depending on the needs and budget of the organization. Your education efforts might include seminars or on the job training for different job techniques. Of course, some careers may call for more advanced or specialized educational opportunities. Development may come in the form of computer-based learning. There are a variety of online learning platforms like Udemy, Linda or LinkedIn Learning. You might find it necessary to create your own specialized classes or to send employees to formal college classes. It is up to your organization to decide what the return on investment will be for each level of form of education. Regardless of what you choose, know that education and training are essential to hiring and retaining the youngest working generations. But this isn't the only thing the new generations want; they want a life.

Work-Life Balance is a concept that might be foreign to the older generations. In the past, the workplace set the work schedule. You worked 8-5 Monday through Friday, with two weeks' vacation and major holidays. The odd day might be negotiated for a child's music recital or for a grandmother's funeral. In recent years however, this tradition has changed at the demand of again the Millennials and Generation Z. Flexibility in work arrangements have since become important to all employees.

In the past, company business could only be done on site since there was no transportability of work materials and office machines. With the advent of internet, cloud computing and video conferencing, professional work has become far more fluid. The 8AM to 5PM tradition can be changed to meet employee needs. Telecommuting has become more and more popular based on these. There are also the rare situations of job sharing, which allows two people to people to share a full-time position. In the end, work-life balance is about trying to identify a win-win situation for an employee to provide valuable labor, while the employer also allows conveniences to the employee can meet other higher order needs. Helping employees find a balance is a great step but you also must help them avoid burnout.

Keeping employees excited and engaged in their work often means helping them to avoid burnout. There are a few different causes of this problem. Employers can be proactive by "right" sizing the job and creating an inventory or what skills and abilities are needed for the job. Many "burned-out," employees report feeling overwhelmed and that they do not have control over their position. This goes back to education and development activities.

There are three reasons for burnout that have a high level of interconnectedness. People become disengaged and fed up with a job when they feel that the organization, they are working with does not have values that coincide with their own. This makes sense when we consider the next common complaint and that is a lack of community. When you work in an organization where the organization does not share your values and you are surrounded by employees who are ostensibly sharing the values with the organization they work with, it makes it difficult to build bonds. This again connects directly with the values you as an organization have instilled in your staff as the organizational culture. If the environment was not well developed and you start bringing in diversity hires, values and community will not align, and your diversity program suffers. We are still not done. Our diverse workforce also seeks to advance in their careers. Have you considered that aspect?

Advancement

Advancement to many seems to be the natural course of employment, seniority and successful work history. True enough in a company that is not celebrating diversity as a value. However, employees from diversity segments see advancement possibilities in an organization for their segment as a bellwether of an organization's commitment to diversity and inclusion. We explored the idea earlier as to how a person would feel coming to an organization in which they were the only one of their kind. Now let's consider a company with a successful record of hiring employees from diversity segments. Now imagine that those diversity hires are never hired into important positions and never find opportunities for advancement. The logical conclusion to this is that it will be difficult to retain diversity hires in such an environment.

There are certainly people who are happy with enjoying job security in the position in which they were first hired. There are not many of those. Most of us want bigger titles and bigger paychecks as our career progresses. Diversity hires are no different. Advancement is also a key in avoidance of burnout which we discussed earlier. Whatever diversity segment we belong to, we are all united with the interest to advance. We must also consider succession planning.

Succession planning is the organized planning for the future leadership of the organization. Our older generation may have advanced and are currently the leaders of the organization, but companies tend to outlive us all, a perfect example of this can be seen in the boardroom of many companies. The classic suit from Brooks Bros. is from a company that was founded in the United States in

1818. For Brook Bros. to continue, to thrive for so long, they underwent continuous organization and understanding that even the most talented and seemingly indispensable employee will someday grow old, retire, or pass away. Who will take their place?

An organization that values diversity and inclusion will consider all employees, identify their needs and goals and mentor those who fit to be a part of succession plan. This inclusion is a real sign that the value of diversity has flowed through the organization. Succession planning is the blueprint as to who will be the leadership of the organization moving forward. With the changing demographics of the United States, the interests and markets will change as well. This means diversity and inclusion is a primary consideration in succession planning. The landscape we see today in the United States proves to be very different in the next 50 years. The company that survives into the future will be able to traverse this tribulation.

A successful business plan is not only about hiring new people and filling the boxes of a diversity segment. It is about making sure your organization can stay abreast of a changing America. It also means creating the largest possible talent pool to find the best candidates for your workplace. If you value sustainable Diversity and Inclusion in your workplace, remember that your internal planning should include retention, development and advancement to fully enjoy the benefits of D&I.

Diversity and Inclusion Training

One of the more unfortunate byproducts of moving from a homogenous organization to a firm that holds diversity is a value is how Diversity and Inclusion is handled within an organization. Since Diversity and Inclusion is a modern idea and as such is not a traditional part of the workplace. Diversity and Inclusion has arrived while more traditional generations still control industry and company organization. For these reasons, diversity and culture is often added as a secondary responsibility for the Human Resources department, since this department is standard in most companies. Human

Resources often considers their primary role first and the role which is most likely to affect what is considered success for an HR Department, that being recruitment and retention. The rest of the facets of Diversity and Inclusion and more importantly the Internal Plan are treated as a tertiary function to be considered when "there's time."

In truth, the internal plan is the responsibility of all departments. The plan will be the practical application of the diversity value and so the organization should be willing to execute their roles in implementation of plan elements. Of these, the delivery of diversity and inclusion training and ongoing communications are perhaps the most important support activities individual departments and leadership must execute. Training our current workforce to face the challenge of Diversity and Inclusion are what make the sustainability of diversity and inclusion possible in a workplace.

Among the most universally important themes that training programs should address, especially in organization that have recently entered into Diversity and Inclusion, are,

Internal Employee Affinity Programs

Sustainability is a common refrain regarding Diversity and Inclusion. This is with good reason. Diversity and Inclusion (D&I) and elements that eventually make up the concept as a whole have bantered about in the American business community since Affirmative Action was implemented in the 1970's. D&I has ebbed and flowed as a point of emphasis during different occasions and then forgotten about as crises of sexual harassment, racial injustice or any variety of -isms waned. The companies that have harnessed the greatest benefits from D&I are also those that have been the most proactive with it and set themselves up for perpetual sustainability. One of the more popular tools to assist in this effort is the formation of Employee Resource Groups (ERGs) or Affinity groups.

ERGs are an effective program that can help maintain D&I as part of a culture and insure sustainability. ERGs are optional and are contingent on the size of your organization. These groups, also known as, Affinity Groups, are formed in organizations based on a loose association of people who share a diversity characteristic. If you choose to start an ERG, one of the more important things to remember is that these groups are a loose affiliation to the diversity group, ergo, an ERG set up for women can also include men and it should perhaps be promoted as accepting men or the concept of D&I starts to erode within these groups.

The ERG is often created to help galvanize the Diversity and Inclusion culture within an organization. They often provide support to diversity community members and employees at large, enhance career development activities as well as assisting in personal development for career advancement. ERGs can be created within an organization to represent any diversity group that feels they could benefit and when such an organization can create a symbiotic relationship within the organization. Successful ERG programs can often be beneficial components to employee recruitment and engagement as they help highlight the company's commitment to D&I ideals.

ERGs can also help nontraditional communities within a workplace to develop leadership skills within the company since ERGs tend to be responsible for their own goals, structure, activities and leadership. They enhance D&I training by keeping it omnipresent as well as making it a more organic social value rather than a forced requirement of employment. ERGs have become ubiquitous in American business culture, finding their way into 90% of all Fortune 500 entities. Because these groups are communities within an organization, it stands to reason, that only companies of enough size and population would have the groups large enough to separate into ERG and therefore benefit from their practice. For this reason, they are a wholly optional tool to benefit an organization seeking to develop their D&I Program.

While your organization may be too small, or simply choose not to create ERGs, you can still create other opportunities to promote D&I within the organization. In fact, it is important to consistently find ways to foster and reinforce the D&I values within your workforce. Many times, diversity groups become invisible due to size or simply indifference due to inattention.

BRIDGING THE GAP: ALIGN AND COMMUNICATE

We have described our plans independently, now we must Bridge the Gaps and bring it all together. We do this through the process of aligning our goals and assessing our progress in plan implementation. This can be done by analyzing appropriate metrics and consider the gamut of diversity segments.

Perhaps the most important aspect of Bridging the Gap is communications. Communications is important in all aspects of the Diversity and Inclusion process. Constant communications of plan elements, goals and even accomplishments are beneficial to the plan. When you communicate the program to the workforce, you reduce anxieties and increase allies. Time to Bridge the Gap!

1. Align

Assessment and Measure

Once you have set up your plan and have your diversity program running smoothly, you may think you are done. In the spirit of Six Sigma and Edwards Deming, the reality is the process is never complete. It is now time to review and assess your plan and consider what has worked for the organization, what failed and what could be improved. The creation of metrics or tools that help us evaluate or monitor our achievements or progress on Diversity and Inclusion within the company is also very important, for that, we need to work closely with the department that takes care of employee satisfaction surveys, climate surveys, scorecards, or other tools. To retain the benefits of Diversity it must achieve sustainability. We can't determine this without assessment.

Metrics

When we consider metrics for assessing our efforts, there are those that give us insight into our hiring and others that express information about inclusion within the organization. Metrics are simply numerical comparisons used to understand your workforce and your further needs. Metrics help human resources professionals and diversity specialists to understand any deficiencies in hiring efforts or whether the organization is meeting obligations at to equal opportunity laws and other mandates. Additionally, metrics help the diversity department consider what goals and initiatives to seek for the coming year. Each company, area and department will need to consider its own goals and targets.

Employment metrics are a powerful first look at whether all facets of your organization have accepted diversity and inclusion as a value. If your HR team or recruitment staff have ignored the value, there won't be a great deal of comparison to look at, things will look about the same year over year. Depending on the malleability, intransigence or simply that management has not enforced accountability on the HR department regarding diversity hiring, it may be necessary to hire a recruiter devoted solely to diversity recruitment efforts. As you consider hiring and inclusion metrics, keep in mind that an organizations choice of measurement is like their own diversity and inclusion fingerprint. The mix of metrics is wholly unique and depends more on how useful the measurements tend to be in advancing your goals.

Some metrics that can be considered for use:

- **Resumes-** Of all the resumes collected for a job, how many of them represented a diversity candidate? How many diversity resumes were handed off to a hiring manager?
- **Interviews-** How many interviews were completed with diversity candidates? What was the percentage of all interviews?
- **Offers-**How many diversity candidates were given offers? What was the percentage of all offers?

- **Hires-**What percentage of all new hires were diverse?
- **Turnover-**What was the turnover rate of diversity hires? How did turnover rate compare versus all new hires in the organization?

Some more specific metric might be used to consider whether diversity and inclusion efforts are effective. These metrics most effectively consider retention. Remember, we can have a diversity program but if we are not creating an environment that will retain minorities, then we are not reaching the prime goal of sustainability.

- **Retention-** Are we consistently retaining diversity hires?

- **Consistency-** Are we making honest efforts throughout all departments to recruit and hire diversity?

- **Conservative Bias-** Many organizations have existed for generations with only men in certain positions. Are we perpetuating biased ideas that inhibit our diversity program?

Still other metrics don't have anything to do with hiring. It can be effective and enlightening to be able to measure the seriousness the organization has regarding diversity and inclusion. We can hire diversity hires, but that is the first step. How committed to diversity is an organization that does not hire diverse employees for important positions? How about if their diversity hires are never promoted? How long would your diversity program continue if diversity segments recognized these issues? We can measure these and offer a picture of how well the organization is doing in this regard.

- **Title and Position-** Do diversity hires have management level positions? Are their diverse hires in important positions in all departments? Is pay similar to that of their peers at the same level?

- **Promotions- Are** we promoting women? Minorities? How many promotions are being offered to minorities and women versus the rest of the organization?

- **Opportunity-** Can minorities and women get access to special jobs? Important projects? What activities can employees create opportunities and learning experiences through?

- **Power Distance-** It is nice to dream that politics, personal charm and proximity to the boss are inconsequential to advancement. We all know that is largely a naïve sentiment. How close do minorities and women get to management and decision makers? How often do they meet?

- **Veterans-** Are we forgetting anyone? In our diversity zeal, the very real segment of age is often forgotten. Are we meeting the needs of our veteran employees? Are we considering the needs of our older employees as we race to the next job fair to pick up the newest crop of college grads?

As you can see, we can create metrics that help us to better understand all aspects of the diversity program we have created. In order to see assess what is working and plan for the future, metrics will help us to have empirical evidence to present to management when we are finding success, when we need to make changes, and whether we need to assess the commitment the organization has to the diversity and inclusion program. The metrics we have discussed are internal metrics to help us assess the internal plan we implemented. Next, we consider the external plan.

Research

A good plan will include research combined with internal assessments.

2. Communications

Your communication department plays an important role in the internal and external plan for Diversity. Communications help to disseminate clear, concise and accessible information about your initiatives and activities to employees. It helps strengthen partnerships with other departments, ERGs, and others internally and externally, and promote an accepting, collaborative and respectful culture in your company.

Communicating your plan to your employees, explaining what will happen, what it means to them and how it will affect the company are all elements that will make the process of implementing the internal plan much easier. Communication of your message should be continuous to your employees. This will make sure the message is received by everyone and reinforce the value proposition to your team. This will become important as changes often create anxiety within teams.

Organizations that have been homogenous for a long time may find it hard to accept the changing climate and the implementation of diversity elements. Regardless of how much your organization reinforces diversity as a value, some employees will never accept diversity and instead will hold their own biases and values as paramount. This is to be expected. Overcommunicating the messages of the plan and their goals to your team can help allay some of the anxiety and derision that may spring forth.

It may also be beneficial to communicate the "Why," of all activities prior to launch. For example, if you plan to celebrate International Women's Day, send out an email or some other communication a week prior that explains what you are doing and why the company will get value from the activity. Of course, you will get some complaint, but others will be happy to see the efforts as well.

Good plans will also include communications from the executive staff to the employees from time to time. A message from the executive should also be included in all external plans as well. The value must be reinforced and continually expressed, or it becomes a cliched concept whose meaning fades with time. The adage out of sight out of mind becomes a maxim with these kinds of philosophies.

A strong communications plan will be proactive in minimizing stress for all stakeholders in the changes you are about to make. Explaining your reasons and goals will ease anxieties and help promote your overall plan since you will now be engaging your entire workforce hitting goals. This is the reason communications is the key element in Bridging the Gap and tying all of your plans together.

The External Plan

The external plan refers to the face you plan to offer to the public. What will your customers and outside stakeholders see from you? What message will a stakeholder carry away with them after an interaction with your organization? Will they believe your commitment to D&I? Will a potential employee believe they would get fair consideration if they were to apply for a job? A good external plan considers the touch points stakeholders have with your organization. Two areas are particularly important and are the most visible space for interaction with customers. The first is customer service, the other is through sales or with the delivery of consumable products and services. Customer service is perhaps the most profound and that which your organization can control most effectively.

Customer Service

Customer service is the area that the customer has the most contact with customers. Special attention and communications must be made focusing on front line staff which channels the internal plan. The externa plan means getting to know the needs of your customers, understanding barriers, motivations, perspectives based on their diverse segments, and analyzing communication methods. Communications and Marketing for your organization should be creating an integrated message for customer service activities.

External awareness has more to do with your customer's perception of diversity and how they will be most greatly affected. When they see themselves represented within your organization or when customers recognize that you understand their diversity segment, then as an organization we have made it known that we are committed to diversity as an organization. How do we do this?

It is important to review every touchpoint between your organization and customers. Can we as an organization, "feel their pain," that is, if we were the customer would you be able to fulfill my needs as a customer adequately and respectfully, in all circumstances? Some of the concepts that should have serious consideration for organizations:

Phone Communications

To many of us this seems like a simple concept. We speak English in the United States, right? Any communications will be in the lingua franca of the country. How respectful is this to the people in your customer base? What are the demographics of your area? Do you have a large contingent of immigrants in your community?

I have often been asked, "Why should we as an organization try to speak any language other than English since our organization requires English to work here?" Whether the customer had to speak English to order your product or if you speak English on the job. Our consideration is the client. What language do they speak? If they do speak a foreign language and English, which do they prefer? Can you effectively explain complex subjects to customers who are not native English speakers? Since it is impossible to know for sure. Why not does something simple like provide a translation service for phone calls? You ensure that your customers understand the product and are comfortable with the service they receive. It also transmits to the stakeholders that you are committed to meeting the needs of all the people you encounter.

Customer Service Staffing

Depending on the area of the country you live in, it is common to see phrases in a foreign language throughout the United States. In Chicago the phrase "Mowimy Po Polsku," is ubiquitous. Throughout the country "Habla Español," is common. In Florida, many signs say "On parle Francais." What language does your organization speak? What are the demographics of your area? Who do you serve? Whose money are you willing to accept as a customer?

When you have a substantial community of people who prefer another language. It might be best to seek out a person who can speak their language. It may increase sales and create an opportunity to hire diverse employees, both of which will signal the diversity commitment you are making. Another area that is not generally considered is the deaf/mute community. How do we help this group? Do we have someone on staff to meet their needs? Is there communication service on staff for this group? These are considerations you should make in your staffing based on your known and possible clientele.

Website

Like our telephone and customer service staffing, the website we use is another touchpoint. It is also easily translatable through a Google widget. This like the direct contact and the phone contact is all about understanding the people may possibly be using your services and trying to make them comfortable. After all, the definition of a gentleman or gentlewoman is a person whose conduct conforms to a high standard of propriety or correct behavior, what is that if it is not helping our customers and everyone around us to feel as comfortable possible.

In the end, it is important to communicate your values to customers and potential recruits. The external environment must be aware of what you are trying to achieve.

Community

Wherever your company is based, you are surrounded by stakeholders, those people who have a stake in the activities of your organization. When your company supports diversity-related interests then it means that your organization has made everyone in the community a stakeholder. D&I initiative in the communities you serve can be combined with a philanthropic purpose and an organizational strategy.

For example, the Employee Resource Groups can provide some volunteer time in the communities. Some events target specific diversity segments such as the Latino outreach, or perhaps Breast Cancer fundraising.

It really depends on the interest of your ERG, the organization and the individual desires of the employees.   The nature of how your organization interacts, their impact with the community and the effect it returns to the organization is all unique. This will reflect executive level devotion to the diversity and inclusion values.

R.A.C.E TO THE FINISH

"R" IS FOR RECOGNITION

"Eureka!" Archimedes screamed as he stumbled on the realization that when he submerged himself in water, the water was displaced, and the water climbed up the sides of the tub. The Greek scholar was so excited by this discovery which would lead to exact weights and measurements, that he ran naked throughout the town. You don't have to be a Greek scholar recognize good work in our lives nor should we run naked through the streets of our neighborhood…that tends to be awkward in the age of #MeToo.

Introspection is required of organizations and leadership in order to realize problems and shortcomings. A wise man once told me, "if you are happy with your limitations… Congratulations- you get to keep them!" Diversity and Inclusion is a common shortcoming for businesses and organizations. My career has been littered with organizations who could not acknowledge their shortfalls. Some finally found a moment of clarity when they took the great leap and recognized diversity in their midst. Others still haven't recognized their failings and continue to pay for their intransigence.

American society has struggled with Diversity and Inclusion since the very beginnings of European settlement in the New World. The first colonies were established by religious orders to segregate themselves and maintain the purity of their brand. The colony of Maryland was set up by Lord Baltimore for Catholic immigrants to the New World. With few Catholics crossing the sea, Maryland also became the first colony to establish up rules to ban Catholics from administrative positions in the colony.

The United States still struggles to overcome the damaging effects and dark legacy of slavery. Women also fought for years to find a place at the table. Many related to Mary Tyler Moore when she threw her hat in the air in Minneapolis. Making progress in these areas requires shaking off the status quo and carving out a new path.

However, for some companies, communities and individuals the new path remains an enigma. They simply cannot recognize the problem.

I encounter this frequently in my profession. Those who have not recognized their need to embrace Diversity and Inclusion as a Value will say something like…. "We don't really care about the color of your skin. We only care that you work hard or that you have the right skill for the job." Another popular catchphrase is, "No one has ever complained about diversity issues here." or "We don't need to talk about diversity because there are not many minorities here." Another common push back, "My company doesn't have to cover special needs because we only have one employee from that group." In each of these instances the organization is not only generally, homogenous in ethnicity, culture, and thoughts but they lack a real strategy and justify it with rigid numbers that create their own barriers to inclusion.

One of my first experiences in dealing with organizations and municipalities who could not see the elephant in the room was in 2006. I had only been in the U.S. for a couple of years and I joined a civic/business organization with chapters throughout the State of Nebraska. One of the chapters was in a town that was undergoing explosive growth and ethnic transformation as meatpacking concerns in the small town attracted thousands of Hispanics during the initial waves of the NAFTA immigration boom of the late 1990's. The parent organization would visit the chapters annually to try and keep them healthy. During one of these visits, a long discussion ensued with the leader of this town's Chapter.

The man lamented, "The whites, they don't let us do anything! We try to have a parade and they send us to the Chamber of Commerce. When we consult the Chamber, they tell us to talk to the city. In the end, they all tell us no!"

Our organization was little help since the city officials would not speak to us either. When they did, their argument was that the organization did not want to follow the rules. This Chapter folded up not long after as there was no resolution. I often thought of this over the years and wondered if the chapter just faced hoops they wouldn't jump through. I have seen multiple times when the immigrant group is being as bad or worse than the most anti-immigrant city administrator, yet the immigrants demand more than the organization of municipality is willing to give.

Recently, I met with the City Administrator of this town. The Whites and Hispanics have essentially drawn a line in the sand that neither of them is willing to cross. A new aspect of ethnic/religious diversity has been added to the mix as the packing plants recruited African refugees to the town.

Since my original visit, the city has been transformed and become almost 85% Latino. Yet, the traditional communities of the town maintain their dominance. The third element were African Muslims who threw their savings into a hat and purchased a long-closed convenience store to use as a Mosque.

The city complained that the Muslims were not considering traffic rules or parking challenges in the city. For the Muslims, that complaint was all too familiar. The Muslims claim that the city is intransigent and offers no solution to the impasse. The city, they say is only pressing them to close their mosque. We ended the conversation with the Administrator expressing that he was not amenable to a meeting nor creating channels of communication with the Muslim group. While I can't be certain who is at fault...I can say that the stakeholders and the leaders in town have not recognized their need to find common ground and change the status quo.

Shortly after the meeting, the Muslim group in town filed suit in Federal Court. The city has taken this as a vindication that they were right in not communicating with this group. That the groups and the ethnic masses now living in the city are the intransigents. It is clear, all parties involved need to realize the need for change in order to move in a more a positive direction.

Sometimes realization comes in an epiphany. Such a revelation is often born from a moment of great stress or conflict. One "aha" moment of mine came from a visit to a local convenience store. My husband and I once owned a gift shop. During that time, we were regulars at a small grocery store/convenience mart. I won't tell you where, but it is in Omaha, NE and it shares its name with a Baby Bear. One night after a long day of selling Peruvian clothes and sundries, we stopped by the store for beer and snacks. This is where the fun begins.

My husband enjoys trying new beers and taking his time making a selection. I was left to find the snacks. I walked around the store picking out little tidbits and when I was done, I went back to the beer aisle and we proceeded to the registers. Waiting near the registers were two police officers. One point from a store clerk and the police surrounded me. The young police officer looked embarrassed as he asked, "Please empty your pockets ma'am."

Scott and I stood incredulously as I emptied my pockets of innocuous things like my wallet and keys, nothing that should not have been there. (Scott had been carrying the snacks.) We walked to the car in a state of shock. I couldn't believe this had just happened to me. It took me minutes to realize that this was a case of profiling. I was the only Latina and the only person of color in that store. Scott returned to the store to ask what the problem was and why this happened. The assistant manager told him that earlier in the night a minority was shoplifting but it wasn't an issue of racism.

Interesting – so the next time a minority, Japanese-Peruvian, walks into the place…you call the police with a complaint of shoplifting…but it isn't racial…Just due diligence? I called a Latino newspaper who graciously published the story in English and Spanish, then I sent the story to the manager of the chain who immediately met with my husband and I. He brought the owner of the franchise with him. It was obvious that they didn't agree with the young man who had accused me of shoplifting. Race was clearly the driving factor in their decision to involve the police since there was nothing that pointed to shoplifting. The owner and his manager expressed their sincere apologies. This experience conjured the epiphany that they needed to recognize their need for change. The status quo for many of their clerks was to meet minorities with suspicion. The owner recognized how faulty that line of thinking was.

It is important to understand that we are all diverse. Diversity is not solely the milieu of minorities; it connects us all in some way. Recognizing the need for change comes organically. It comes from seeing the changes happening in your community and having an interest in getting ahead of the issue. Nebraska has been transformed through immigration over the past 20 years. City after city and town after town have seen their demographics transformed. Schools are filled with children and boarded up main streets have been reinvigorated with entrepreneurship.

An influx of population unlike yourself can be unnerving. It can bring stress and conflict as cultures clash. The concept of Diversity and Inclusion does not seek to change your mind about your personal values. However, the business benefits of diversity are clear. Therefore, in our business lives we must find a way to recognize diversity has been always present in our lives and we must find a way to work within that reality. The easiest way is to simply respect those around us.

Maybe your organization or company already has a Diversity and Inclusion plan. Some of those plans may have been in place since the 1990's. One organization I consulted with to revamp their plan had groups of employees who were extremely defiant with any changes to the existing plan. Why? Because the plan, which was crafted during the Clinton presidency, really demanded nothing of the people within the organization. A quick survey of the employees revealed that the diversity program was either largely forgotten or was unknown to newer employees.

This is another aspect of recognition. Older plans trended toward the rudimentary. They were focused on old affirmative action guidelines which did not offer a full spectrum of what diversity in business really entails. Diversity includes visible and invisible differences (gender, race, generation, religion, values, experiences, perspectives, the way we solve problems, how we make decisions, etcetera). Diversity is a very broad concept that we all know exists but tend to avoid facing by developing reasons why we don't need to work on it "right now."

A perfect example of this occurred when I was working with a small city in central Nebraska. In order to help understand where their organizational readiness was, we created an organizational survey. The results were clear. Seventy percent of employees stated that Diversity and Inclusion were NOT needed. Despite the large number who said there was no need for a new program, more than 60% had some sort of complaint regarding the treatment of a diverse segment within the company. Some lamented how disconnected to decisions they became as they neared retirement. Others noted their displeasure with how they had been treated as members of the LGBTQ+ community. Another group felt more women were needed in the company. Yet, 70% believed that a new Diversity program was illegitimate. Essentially, the organization was simply going through the motions and using the right language when needed. They had not maintained Diversity and Inclusion as a corporate value.

Earlier in my career, I worked for a very famous children's organization. Based on the many values this organization tries to teach young people, one would assume that the mutual respect rooted in Diversity and Inclusion would naturally be one of those values. Unfortunately, Diversity and Inclusion seemed to be a foreign concept. Sometimes, it is the lower level employees who say and do things they shouldn't do, that might be accepted as a bad hire or the need for intensive supervisory admonishment. What happens when the problem is the executive staff?

I was hired to manage a part of an outreach program aimed at helping Black and Hispanic boys. I took care of the Hispanic side and I had a counterpart for the Black neighborhoods. As I worked the community I was assigned, I was inundated by rumors of the person who had filled my position prior to me. It was a Mexican man who I was acquainted with. There were allegations of racism and ill will towards the organization. Finally, I went to visit this person. He told me that his supervisor called him a "Wet Back!" This is an older pejorative that some may not know. It disparagingly describes a Hispanic person with a "wet back," insinuating that they had waded over the Rio Grande river as an illegal immigrant. This may seem mild but for many Latino's this is as painful as any of the classic epithets that may have more recognition. This was not the only incident of something like this happening.

Some of the schools I worked with were home to some very troubled boys. One day, I had a particularly aggressive boy create problems at a meeting. I told him to go home. He was obviously very upset. When I returned to the office, my boss confronted me and asked if I had admonished a boy and called him "a punta," (pronounced Poon-Tah). Why would I call anyone a punta? The word means edge or corner. What the child's white, English speaking mother was trying to insinuate is that I had called her boy a "puta." Which I would never do to anyone, let alone a young boy. The word "puta," is a Spanish slang word for prostitute. The form with an "a" at the end is used only for women.

My black female counterpart who handled the African American community accompanied her boys on a campout. When she arrived, her supervisor gave her a walkie-talkie and got busy working with the children. In the meantime, the supervisor forgot about the walkie-talkie and started bantering back and forth about both the children and my friend, whom they called the "N" word, multiple times. My friend sat helplessly as her supervisor abused her with some of the vilest racial language imaginable. Then these adults went back to the task of trying to form young minority children. Children they said they wanted when they created the special program in an effort to connect and impact these communities.

This organization has been through a variety of social problems over the past several years. It was clear from these episodes that they had not recognized the issues in front of them. It was obvious they understood that racial diversity was something they wanted to achieve in their organization but they were oblivious of how they were treating their counterparts. One of their errors was never actually learning about the community they hoped to work with. Instead they would simply hire people that matched the race of the target audience and sent them out to build a market. The organization didn't even respect the people they hired.

In the end, the organization was sued for the verbal assault against the young, black woman. It was an unfortunate end to the situation and meant that an organization to help young boys was forced redirect funds to pay the settlement. Their inability to recognize, or perhaps refusal to make the changes diversity requires, created a terrible environment.

Racism and racist episodes are not solely isolated to whites and their organizations. While there are some social justice definitions that describe that racism can only exist when the purveyor has both prejudice and power, for me, this definition seems to be a way for some minorities in the United States to maintain racist attitudes toward whites while claiming it is impossible. The racial attitudes in the United States are strange to me and have often confused me.

In Peru, I grew up with many of the racial variations that exist in the US with much less of the negative feelings that separate us. We have Afro-Peruvians, Japanese-Peruvians, Chinese, Indians, Mestizos, Spaniards, and yes, even whites. All of these people groups largely live without rancor. Imagine my surprise when I moved to the United States and faced a country that looked at me suspiciously despite immigrating here with a legal visa.

It was interesting when I found my first job in the United States. I worked at a fast food restaurant where my fellow employees were mostly black women. They looked different than the black women in Peru. At the time, it seemed as if they started off at one volume and continued to increase with each word to the end of a conversation. This group that I worked with spoke about any topic. But any filter they possessed seemed to die when they walked through the door.

So, I became the topic of conversation when I started dating a black man. How is a Latina supposed to be with a Black man? Some left it at a bit of ribbing but, for others, my relationship was a serious problem.

"You need to be with your own kind." They would say.

I failed to understand why it was their business. Really it was a form of racism and certainly not a discussion for work. The workforce is a lot different from what I am dealing with today but it was a situation where my co-workers had a low education and were suspicious of people outside their own communities.

While this is not true of all communities of any race, this group had no realization that their prejudice was detrimental to themselves and it made them victims of their anger. This is largely true every time racist activities take place. The people doing it may see themselves as right at the time, maybe they feel vindicated for a moment. The onlookers see them as unfortunate people who are low social status. This seems to be a maxim that runs true regardless of the skin color of the victim or aggressor.

Sometime later, I was mentoring teens through an organization. This activity brought me in contact with several African-Muslim teens. By this time, I was married to my husband, a white man. It didn't really matter to me but again it piqued the emotions of others. One young lady I was mentoring, saw pictures of my family that included my husband. With a disappointed and then incredulous look she asked, "Ms. Yesenia, why in the world would you choose a white man?! Don't you know they are all racist?"

That day I was also disappointed since it was so personal. My husband didn't hate anyone. Least of all for something so trivial as the color of their skin. I asked her how she came up with such a thought. "My mother told me," she replied.

I thought about that definition of prejudice and power and thought how if it were true, she would almost be doomed to a marginalized existence being a black Muslim girl. I told her that obviously my husband isn't racist since we were together. I spoke and tried to reason with her. I received more than a few eye rolls. I could tell the value was just too instilled for an impromptu mentoring discussion to break through the monolithic cultural wall that had been constructed. I did my best and hopefully my words ring true someday.

Years after ending that project, I bumped into one of the girls and their mother. My husband and I were together. The two black ladies happily ran to me and hugged me, they talked to me and excitedly told me about their lives. My husband stood dutifully silent, waiting for an acknowledgement that he existed. He smiled and nodded his head. When the conversation ended, they said goodbye to me while their mother gave a slight icy nod at my husband as she walked away. It was evidence to me that the prejudice they felt still survived. They were not using critical thinking and chose to believe all whites were somehow a menace. The realization that every member of a race is not the same is an important distinction. We are all different even among different groups. What is important to remember is even with our differences, we are more connected than we may see in our superficial variations.

Takeaways

- As obvious as it might be for a D&I Practitioner that all organizations need to consider and implement policy that stresses diversity and inclusion as corporate values – for a myriad of reasons, your organization and its employees may not think they need a D&I policy.

- The D&I Officer often must help their target audience RECOGNIZE the deficiencies and sometimes the delinquencies in their present activities.

- Several organizations have had a Diversity program for decades. However, they were just going through the motions. They never realized a need for D&I as a value.

- Make sure your audience has a definition of diversity they can understand. Don't assume they know. If

you are taking over a program, know the definition
the organization works under,

- Recognition sometimes arrives like a lightning strike
while other times it arrives like a glacier.

"A" IS FOR ACCEPTANCE

"The way I see it, if you want the rainbow, you have to put up with the rain."   Dolly Parton

This is almost a maxim when it comes to accepting things that are universally considered a positive thing. However, when it comes to value or change, humans trend towards intransigence. Even when they realize there is a need, they will rationalize how the old way is sufficient. They will fight the plan as inadequate or unnecessary.

When we challenge long held opinions, we generally meet obstructions because humans have a hard time tapping into their critical thinking skills. Instead they take new concepts as an affront to their value systems. It takes a leader to move a group past this impediment.

Recognizing the need for D&I is an important step; perhaps the most important. However, it is the first step. Now D&I has to function within the organization. How do we align the organization with the benefits of D&I? How do we get organizational "buy-in" for diversity and inclusion efforts? How do find acceptance for our organization?

First, we must define what it means to accept D&I as a value. An organization accepts diversity and inclusion when all facets of the organization have implemented the aspects and programs designed to ensure all diversity sectors are considered and included in hiring and decision-making processes. Organizations with leadership or employee population that has little connection with diverse communities or has been imbrued with a politically charged concept of what diversity is will find the process of acceptance to be a more difficult process.

During part of my diversity journey, I implemented D&I programs with a non-profit organization that that wanted to work on "making everyone feel welcome and happy to work there." It was the first time the process had been undertaken at this location and like many of my partnerships it was fraught with early misunderstandings and zeitgeist that diversity was a "political concept meant to appease minorities." This is a common issue in the corporate world.

Soon after creating a D&I training session and distributing it out to the employees, I received an email from a frustrated employee. For the sake of this example, we'll call this employee "Bob." In sum, Bob was compelled to tell me that the diversity process was a fraud and he did not think it was a valid work concern. Bob's choice of words were not as professional as this. However, it was clear that his e-mail was not written to be constructive. My rule is to reply ONCE to anyone sending me such correspondence. I thanked Bob for writing me. I asked him his concerns and reiterated the true meaning and benefit of diversity to the organization.

Bob replied…with less eloquence and less professional language. Bob explained that he had seen diversity in action just that day. He went on to describe a racist trope about a lazy convenience store employee who made the other employee work while he sat and ate watermelon and fried chicken. I did not respond because nothing constructive could be derived from the conversation. I recognized that this peculiar individual had not accepted that he was surrounded by diversity and that it had to be fostered and managed.

What does it mean to accept diversity and Inclusion? In step one we recognized that diversity exists and that the concept includes all of us, but recognition is passive. Now we need to have action. Now we must ACCEPT Diversity and Inclusion. We have to start tending the environment that will allow diverse communities to be a part of the conversation. Acceptance means that voices that once were whispers or worse, silent, now can at least offer a position on the effects of decisions made by firms or communities.

The first step is identifying and accepting that you do, in fact, have minorities of all types in your community or organization. Take a look around and be observant. Who is African? Sometimes it is easy to tell. The stereotypical African dress and black skin might tell you they are African. But what about a South African? An Afrikaner? How do we tell? They are English or Dutch in origin, so they are Caucasian but still African.

How about a Latino? Inclusion for them is easy, isn't it? Just accept that you must provide Spanish translation to everything, right? What does a Latino look like? You can always pick them out... "they all look the same!" These questions and ideas are why acceptance is so difficult. The answers to diversity and inclusion are not simple.

Not all Latinos speak Spanish. If they come from Guatemala, there is a good chance that they speak Spanish...or Mayan. If they are Brazilian, they tend to speak Portuguese. Peruvian? Spanish, Quechua, Aymara or dozens of jungle languages. And what does a Latino look like? Are they short with black hair and dark skin? Are they tall, thin with hazel eyes and white skin? Do they have Asian features? Acceptance means we don't know what we might be facing but we know it exists and we know we must prepare.

In the recognition section we noted that every situation is different for every community. When you accept Diversity and Inclusion as a value, your approach to achieving D&I in your organization are as varied as a snowflake. Diversity and Inclusion is not for the squeamish. When you make the choice to move toward this value, it means a lot of discernment and introspection as an organization. Acceptance means that you recognize that your best interest is served by developing an organization and community that is respectful and inclusive to all diversity segments. Even those you may not agree with personally or spiritually.

In the past 20 years or so, homosexuality has become an accepted aspect of society. It is no longer spoken of in the hushed tones of the past. Our media is replete with examples of homosexuals and their achievements. Conservative estimates say 6-

10% of Americans are homosexual. That means that if you live in a small town of 500 people, there is a very real possibility that 50 of them are homosexual. Even the most conservative and highly religious towns are highly likely to have a population there.

The same issue exists for transgender. Estimates say that this group represents 0.6% of the population. That means in that same small town of 500 there are an estimated 3 transgender individuals. You may not know any homosexuals or transgender individuals personally or may never have attended school with any…but do they simply refuse to admit it? Are they too afraid to deviate from the homogeneity of the community?

When your community accepts diversity and inclusion as a value and accepts the duties that go along with it, the change in attitudes and behaviors will bring diversity out of the woodwork…the diversity you originally thought did not exist. You might have known about them or forgot they existed, maybe they just kept to themselves to avoid negativity. Acceptance means that your community and organization are ready to make the changes necessary to make Diversity and Inclusion work.

Takeaways:

- Acceptance is necessary for the process to work. It is the step that means upcoming changes will be successful.

- To accept diversity and inclusion means all diversity segments. Accepting diversity means recognizing it as a value.

- Never believe that diversity doesn't exist. We are all involved in diversity. Even the rarest of unicorns should be considered when creating a diversity program.

"C" FINDING COMMONALITIES

Your audience has recognized that diversity exists. They know what the concept of diversity is and what it entails. After recognizing diversity, the arbiters of the organization or community had to accept that a new reality was needed. They accepted that the status quo was not sustainable and that it was necessary to tap into all available talent pools. Once we have reached this point, we must break down opposition even further.

This is not aggressive; it is not a purge! Our actions are to incentivize change. We incentivize change by identifying commonalities. This is not an easy task! We all have similar trials and tribulations. They are similar but rarely the same. Because of this, those that want to remain opposed to change, and opposed to diversity initiatives, will rarely accept any commonality that can be cast away through rhetorical flourish.

When I started my work in rural Nebraska, it was very difficult for some communities to find commonalities within the various diversity segments in their midst. It seems almost instinctive that we find differences among people, especially when "race" is such an easily identifiable characteristic or when current philosophies and societal problems color the thinking of a large part of the community.

One example of this occurred when a community I was working with made a commitment to connect with the Latino population in the community. It was refreshing to see the traditional residents of the community seeking inclusion and an effort to connect with people that were not traditional residents of the community. Despite the initial spirit of inclusion, some of the community created artificial barriers based on stereotypes and tired biases.

One of the meetings was spent considering reasons why the Hispanic community was reluctant to be involved with traditional events in the town. Several group members complained that Latinos are never willing to support their community efforts or willing to learn. Others assumed the Latino community was undocumented and didn't care about the activities of the community. Still, others felt it too difficult to involve this group, because they were uneducated, poor and didn't speak the language.

The meeting changed directions when the group learned more about Latino culture. It is always important to have representatives of specific groups to explain misconceptions. By the end of the meeting, the majority understood that the Latino community, especially first-generation immigrants do not have a high concept of community involvement. Spending time at a board meeting takes time from their work, household chores or family business. Giving back to the community is not common in third world countries like Peru or Mexico, unless it is related to a religion or church. Not to say that volunteerism is nonexistent, but it is not a common activity in those places. Consequently, community involvement is a challenge for this group.

For the second generation of Latinos, raised in the U.S., community involvement is something they have been raised with and have been introduced to in school. This generation of Latinos will help make community inclusion more viable.

It is important to remember that when you engage in diversity and inclusion that too many times conflicts between racial groups are chalked up solely to racism. It is often unfair to describe these issues as racism or discrimination. It has more to do with a lack of knowledge of their target market or flaws in logic regarding their opposites. This phenomenon is NOT solely a problem for whites and inclusion into predominantly white communities. I have seen many instances of people at all professional strata and in all minority groups who failed to understand different cultures and racial groups.

I was working on creating a coalition of a variety of different groups in the city to help me meet goals I created. The organization assembled a team and we scheduled a meeting. As this chapter states, my philosophy in approaching groups, especially those possibly opposed to me, is to find commonalities. I presented my plan to this organization who was dedicated to making the lives of Hispanics in the community easier. After a long discussion about the strategy I planned to take, the plan was received with disappointment. Since I was only seeking support for a plan that belonged to me and my organization, this response was surprising to me.

I asked the group what problem they saw with the plan. One of the gentlemen spoke up, he said, "You are brainwashed! You think too white!" This really surprised me. In my life I had been accused of many things but never that I thought like a White-American. I didn't really know what this person meant by this. Does a white person think in sepia-tone?

"What do you mean?" I asked.

"When you want to get something from White people, you have to be militant and demand it! They are racist against anyone who is not of their own kind!"

It did not change my mind, I decided to look at this as a challenge. By creating success through finding commonalities, I would educate my own race to understand that our opposition is almost never truly racist. If they were, what is the likelihood that they would even talk to us? I was successful in the goals I set forth that day. I think, at least in this community, the Hispanic community has embraced the RACE philosophy as a plan of action. I know, that the philosophy of militant antagonism exists and is still being pushed in different organizations throughout the state.

Perhaps one of the most powerful examples of creating commonalities comes from an incredibly successful project I was able to implement in one community. It was created, again through commonalities. Two major communities in this community struggled to find common ground and this had persisted for a long time. One thing that unites us all in this life is work and money. The commonality we identified was what became known as the Microbusiness Program.

The Microbusiness Program was a perfect program because it united all the stakeholders. The organization I worked with was excited about helping various members of the community start businesses because this helped grow their own interests. The various diversity segments of this community saw this as an opportunity to create business that would help them provide a better living for their families. The program was presented in both Spanish and English allowing virtually all people in the community to partake in the program.

When we first set the program up, we had an abundance of organizations and companies that offered space and time to allow us to meet. Since new business is an opportunity for virtually all stakeholders, we were also blessed with many knowledgeable presenters. The common ground of creating new entrepreneurs means more people who have money to grow the local economy.

Programs like these mean commonalities must be identified and presented to all involved on a long-term basis. Since the project is ongoing, this means the process of finding commonalities will be long-term. Commonalities must be identified through different organizations, different participants and perhaps different communities as you find success and the opportunity expands. The amazing thing about finding commonalities? Everyone gets what they want!

Outside projects will always need coordination of different groups and people to reach the goals of a project. You might ask if this program will work within a workplace and the answer is a resounding YES! When asked this question, it makes me think about how I started. I was with an organization, I was new, in a small town. I did not have any friends or family to connect with. Due to my job title and the philosophical difficulties that diversity and inclusion often creates, I found myself a kind of stranger in a strange land. It was sort of up to me to make a change.

Within my company, I went on a quest to identify partners and visionaries that could help me reach the goals the organization had for me in addition to my own. Something to remember, when you are working on a project that affects the entire organization, one person cannot hope to be the arbiter that seeks to create a complete value change in an organization. For me, it meant discovering change agents in several different departments throughout the company. I needed an ally in communications to get my message out to the entire organization. Legal counsel was a must since my work connected to human resources. As I went on, I kept finding the allies I needed through commonalities they had with my message and the comradery of employment at the same firm.

Takeaways:

- Identify the things that bring communities together. Economic concerns are the most natural since it binds us all.

- There are no cultural loyalties. By seeking a commonality with one cultural group, it does not mean you are being disloyal to your own. A commonality means you are doing what is best for both groups or numerous groups.

- Finding commonalities is critical since it develops trust between disparate groups. Commonalities are critical for inclusion since we must feel like our opposite has some relationship to common issues.

"E": EVALUATING YOUR PROGRESS

The organization or community that you are working with has realized a need for diversity. They have accepted the fact that changes are necessary and the reasons for them. We have identified commonalities between disparate groups so we can break down barriers. We think we are making progress...but how do we know? The final turn on the track is to Evaluate our progress! How are we doing? Is our goal in sight?

It is important to evaluate your progress regularly throughout the RACE format. Have you helped all the right decision makers realize the benefits of diversity and inclusion? If not, what can you do to improve on this? The same can be said regarding Acceptance. What do we do when the people we want to reach aren't really accepting the reasons for change? How do we improve the level of acceptance?

Perhaps the most important aspect of sustainability is creating commonalities. If we have Realization and Acceptance but have not identified the Commonalities, it ends up keeping people at arm's length. It means you have people who tolerate diversity in their workplaces and communities but without commonalities...inclusion is absent. When there are not enough meaningful commonalities, no trust is created. Why would the dominate group accept the input of a minority group without something that binds them together? When working through the RACE process, it is important to continually consider and evaluate the commonalities that have been raised. Have they been effective in bringing groups together? If not, which ones might still be considered? You can't really overdo it here. Most groups who see each other as oppositional do so because they don't understand their counterparts. Continue to evaluate and adapt your activities to improve on the tenets of the RACE format.

Takeaways:

- Always evaluate and reevaluate what you are doing. That means your success and along with your deficiencies.

- Modify your activities even if you are repeating successful activities from another organization or community.

AT THE END, THIS CAN BE YOU!

Real Stories in the Good Life

The cleaning lady is not always your Latina neighbor.

It seems a lot of the most important parts of my life in the United States have been tainted by unfortunate instances of clumsy behavior that compelled me to my current career. I had just signed the lease on my first apartment in the United States. It was my first time living on my own. It was an urban loft, an old converted warehouse with exposed brick.

It was an exciting day when I got the keys and could finally start filling my new place. It was a thrilling time for me and I decided to bring a friend. My best friend and I were still single ladies and so we always dressed to impress. We slowly ambled up the stairs talking loudly to each other, excited about the possibilities. We drew the attention of two ladies in the hallway.

The young woman waved us into the hallway. I looked at my friend who shrugged. We followed her and watched as she opened a small door. "I am so glad you are here. We have had such a hard time keep cleaning ladies."

My friend and I stood for a moment, shocked at the assumption until my friend burst out with a hysterical cackle, which brought me to laughter. The young woman realizing her error slowly shut the door to what I believe was a broom closet.

"You aren't the cleaning ladies?" she asked. "No, I came to see my new apartment," I replied.

Based on where the apartment was and the usual clients. The likelihood is that the woman assumed that we did not live there. We must have been employees. I was not angry. Today, it serves as a lesson that things have changed. The diversity of the country and certainly the State of Nebraska has changed. The old stereotype of Latinas as poor, menial laborers, living in substandard housing has given way to professionals of all types inhabiting all areas.

Some things take a long time to change, especially when the victims of bad behavior help continue the behavior. I have made many friends and connections in my career. I find it fascinating when some of the strongest, most accomplished women I know share stories of the problems they have faced. One of these women was a supervisor of mine. She told me about how the organization had originally been almost 100% male.

Twenty years before, they started hiring women for some administrative positions. As they progressed, they hired women for numerous positions including management level. In any organization with more than three people there are meetings. This organization was lousy with meetings. Of course, women started being a part of those meetings and if you have ever been in a corporate meeting there are always two constants. A person who takes minutes and coffee.

My colleague explained her experiences in the male dominated culture. In every meeting, she was tasked with preparing coffee and taking notes. Despite the fact that she was supposed to be in management, her voice was rarely heard. Her ideas were often glossed over. Her biggest regret? Much of the fault for this was her own.

She lacked confidence in a male dominated workplace and when she attended meetings, she tried to be agreeable with the men in the organization. It got her caught in a vicious cycle she could get out of. Her problem is a common story among American offices. A woman is asked to do a menial task that anyone could do. When it happens the first time, it becomes tradition and the woman becomes trapped.

My colleague would go to meetings and bring coffee or take notes while several male employees below her on the totem pole were expected to offer their opinion at the meeting. I talked with her about the situation and she said it always bothered her a little. But her nature was to be motherly and in a small town, it almost takes on traditional gender roles, regardless of the tasks being completed.

Sometimes, we must think about even the small things. Those aspects of work life that we often disregard as trivial. Do we share the menial duties or do we depend on someone else to do it? Does dependence on this person or persons diminish their ability to be heard? Are they included? Remember that appealing to traditional gender roles is not a position we hold at work. It is a tough issue and it means a lot of mindfulness but in the end, the solution may simply be…. take turns.

Ready to be Heard!

Luisa met Joe through a work colleague. It was a brief meeting and Luisa thought nothing of it. Joe was a nice man quiet but, otherwise, unremarkable. The next time Luisa bumped into Joe, he was reading a flyer on the wall and Luisa walked up and said, "Good morning Joe." Joe did not move at all. Luisa spoke a little louder, "Good morning," he didn't move but a moment after, he glanced over. He came to shake Luisa's hand and he said something that seemed garbled. It was at that moment, Luisa realized he was deaf. In the previous introduction, the colleague who introduced them did not mention the fact and their communication was brief.

Joe tried to motion and tell her he was deaf. Luisa was mortified that she had not known. She started to discuss his work with him and how long he had been with the firm. They struggled with conversation until he took her to his desk where he had a pencil and paper. He scribbled out his words and she was again surprised to learn he had worked at the company for three decades.

It was a surprising revelation because Luisa had been creating videos to help train employees on a variety of topics. Luisa had made no effort to make sure the training videos were closed captioned for the hard of hearing. It had not occurred to her that it was necessary to create solutions for the deaf community. Luisa had not done her due diligence in this regard. She was disappointed in herself.

After this meeting, Luisa had a discussion with her supervisor who told her that Joe tends to reject any actions to assist her and so the organization finds way to offer the gist of anything that the other employees are told. She went back to Joe to ask what solutions he received for training. He showed me a variety of written manuals that provide pure information, there was never any contextual information offered to help with understanding. Luisa left with the realization that as an organization, they had failed, but it was time to do better! Joe had not been included in anything with the organization for most of his career there.

Luisa immediately contacted communications and asked for captioning in their videos. While the supervisor was correct, Joe did not like extra help based on his hearing loss, the company was complacent in simply going along with this. Joe provided his labor but was never included in the organization. Joe survived in a kind of limbo.

It is important that we don't forget that we need to bring everyone into the fold, we must respect our employees and neighbors. The deaf community is another diversity segment that must be considered.

www.ingramcontent.com/pod-product-compliance
Lightning Source LLC
Chambersburg PA
CBHW052142270326
41930CB00012B/2990

* 9 7 8 0 5 7 8 6 2 9 3 2 2 *